Contents

Meet the cyclists	4
Starting out	6
Track cycling	8
Road racing	12
Mountain bike racing	13
Cyclo-cross	15
BMX	16
In training	18
Lifestyle	22
Races	24
Sporting heroes	26
Plans and ambitions	28
Glossary	30
Find out more	31
Index	32

Meet the cyclists

Most people learn to ride a bike at some time in their life. Cycling is a great way of getting around, as well as a good way to keep fit and healthy. Riding to school instead of going in the car could be good for you and for the environment.

As well as being a useful way of getting from one place to another, cycling is also a fun hobby and a competitive sport. There are lots of skills and tricks that you can learn on a **bicycle motocross (BMX)** or a mountain bike. Or you may prefer the fast, exhilarating sport of cycle racing.

In this book you will meet four cyclists who are training to compete in top-level events. They will share some of their experiences, such as how they got started in the sport, and what made them want to compete. They will also tell you about the training and discipline it takes to race, and what it feels like to win.

John Paul

I am 16 years old and I compete in track events. I am currently in the sixth form at school, working towards A levels in chemistry, physics, biology and PE.

*It was watching Chris Hoy win the **Kilo Time Trial** (see page 9) at the Athens Olympics in 2004 that inspired me to try cycling. I started track cycling at Palmer Park Velo in Reading on Saturday mornings, and after a few goes I absolutely loved it and knew that this was what I wanted to do as a main sport. This year I have won 13 gold and two silver medals. I am also the Under-16 (U16) national record holder for the 200m and 500m Time Trial.*

Hannah Barnes

I am 16 years old and I compete in road, track and mountain bike events. I am at school doing my A levels. I like going out with friends and going to see films in the cinema. I also like music and keeping up with the latest fashion.

*I have got 12 national championships to my name, including the British National Time Trial Championship. I've won that for three years now. In 2009, I won the women's **Cyclo-cross** National Trophy Series.*

TRAINING TO SUCCEED

Cycling

Rita Storey

FRANKLIN WATTS
LONDON • SYDNEY

First published in 2010 by
Franklin Watts
338 Euston Road
London NW1 3BH

Franklin Watts Australia
Level 17/207 Kent Street
Sydney NSW 2000

Words in **bold** are in the glossary on page 30.

Series editor: Julia Bird
Art director: Jonathan Hair

Series designed and created for Franklin Watts by Storeybooks.
Designer: Rita Storey
Editor: Nicola Barber
Photography: Tudor Photography, Banbury (unless otherwise stated)

Picture credits
Jasper Juinen/Getty Images p12, Steve Parsons - Pool/Getty Images p26 Feng Li/Getty Images p27: Larry Hickmott pp 3, 9, 10, 15, 24 and 29.

Thanks to CK Flash and everyone at the Peckham BMX club, Shane Benson and the staff at the Palmer Park Velodrome and Tre Whyte, Alice Barnes, Hannah Barnes and John Paul for their participation in the book.

A CIP catalogue record for this book is available from the British Library.

Dewey classification: 796.6'2
ISBN: 978 0 7496 9540 8

Printed in China

Franklin Watts is a division of Hachette Children's Books, an Hachette UK company.
www.hachette.co.uk

Tre Whyte

I am 16 years old and I am a BMX rider. I'm at college doing GCSEs. BMX takes up most of my time, so I don't really have any other hobbies. I used to do kung fu and football, but for the last two years I've just done BMX.

I was British Champion in my age group in 2008, and second in 2009.

Alice Barnes

I am 14 years old and I compete in road, track and mountain bike events. I am in year 10 at school and I took PE, geography and drama for my options.

I don't have time for other hobbies, my life is pretty much all cycling, but I don't mind because I enjoy the training sessions and I've made lots of friends through cycling.

Tre (above), Hannah (bottom left), John, (middle) and Alice (right) have all proved that they have the potential to become world-class cyclists.

Starting out

Young people often try out a number of different sports before they find one that they really enjoy. Once someone decides to take up a sport seriously, how much they achieve is down to a combination of talent, dedication – and good luck.

Cycling in school

Most cyclists first learn about road safety and cycling skills at school. Bikeability is the name of the cycling training scheme designed to give young cyclists the skills and confidence to ride their bikes on the roads. As part of the National Standards for cycle training, it is taught in schools across England and Wales. Scotland also has a similar scheme.

I was ten when I took up cycling as a hobby, and my sister Alice was seven. When we moved to Towcester we saw a sign at the bike shop for a club that had training and youth races on Wednesday nights. We went along and enjoyed it, so have carried on ever since.

My sister and I were told that we could do well in the sport because we were both strong. We started competing and found out that they were right!

Cycling clubs

To learn the skills of competitive cycling you need to join a cycling club. There are many different types of cycling you can get involved in, and most clubs specialise in one particular type. For example, BMX clubs have a BMX track to train on. Most clubs run taster sessions or encourage you to go along to watch before you decide which type of cycling is right for you.

Young BMX riders listen to their coach before they compete in a race.

When you become a club member you can take part in competitions organised by the club.

Going further

If a rider has talent they may want to take part in more than club competitions. In Great Britain there are several programmes designed to help talented cyclists reach their full potential.

Go-Ride Go-Ride introduces young cyclists to the full range of different types of cycling – BMX, cyclo-cross, mountain biking, road and track riding. Linked to a number of schools and clubs, the scheme helps cyclists under 16 move on from school and club cycling to competing in regional competitions.

Talent Team Programme Riders who show promise may be invited to join the Talent Team for 13 to 17 year olds. On this programme they have a personal coach who arranges their training and racing.

This is done to fit around school work and exams. They also attend training camps during the school holidays. Hannah and Alice are on the Talent Team Programme. Hannah also rides with a British **elite** road race team.

Olympic Development Programme If riders show continued dedication and talent, they may be asked to move on to the Olympic Development Programme. This is for riders between 16 and 18 years old. Their racing and training programme will still be designed to fit in with school work and exams. At this stage they may represent Great Britain abroad. John and Tre are both on the Olympic Development Programme.

U23 Academy Programme Once they are offered a place on this programme, riders usually begin full-time residential training.

Olympic Podium Programme For the few who make it to the very top, this programme funds all their physical and psychological training as well as providing clothing, travel and equipment – everything they need to win!

I've done other sports like football, rugby, badminton and athletics. Dad has always encouraged me just to have a go and enjoy it.

*I was 12 years old when I took up cycling. I love the excitement of racing and the **adrenalin**-rush you get from speeding around the track, as well as the way the track feels as you go round the bends.*

My dad is a BMX rider and still comes to the club on Saturdays to train and take part in races.
My older brother is on the Podium Programme and my younger brother is doing really well at BMX too, so it runs in the family.

Track cycling

Track racing can take place outdoors or indoors. Outdoor tracks are concrete or tarmac. Indoor tracks are oval and made of wood. Tracks are banked (they have sloping sides). For top-level indoor events, cyclists ride on wooden tracks between 250m and 500m long. These are called velodromes.

Aerodynamics

As a cyclist moves forward, he or she has to cut though the air in front of the bike (known as **wind resistance**). The faster a cyclist goes, the harder this becomes – the difference in **air pressure** in front of and behind the cyclist literally 'drags' him or her back (**aerodynamic drag**). To combat this drag effect, cyclists make themselves and their bikes as thin and pointed as possible to cut through the air. Track bikes are designed to be very narrow. They have an extra set of bars (called skis) so that riders can tuck their elbows in during a race and make themselves narrow, too. A cyclist's track helmet is designed to allow the air to flow over it smoothly. Even the suits worn by riders are designed to be sleek and **aerodynamic**.

Types of track events

There are two groups of track events – **sprint** and **endurance**. Sprint events are short, fast and furious. Endurance events are longer and require great **stamina**.

Sprint events

Team Sprint A race where teams of three enter, but only one rider finishes. Two teams start at the same time on opposite sides of the track. After one lap the first rider (rider 1) of each team pulls out. At the end of the second lap the front rider in each team pulls out (rider 2). This leaves one rider from each team to finish the race (rider 3). The job of the first two

John takes part in an Individual Sprint race at a velodrome.

Track bikes
*Track bikes have neither brakes nor **gears**. They have a **fixed wheel**, so the cyclist has to pedal all the time. The speed is controlled entirely by pedalling. Because of their design, track bikes require a lot of energy to get them going at the start of a race.*

I concentrate on the sprint disciplines such as Match Sprint, Kilo (Time Trial), Keirin and Team Sprint.

I prefer the buzz you get from the short, explosive sprint events. They suit me better than the long endurance events, which could be 120 laps compared to three for a Match Sprint.

A group of riders in a Keirin race get ready for a fast sprint when the motorbike pacer (derny) pulls off the track.

riders is to get the speed of the other riders up as high as possible so that the third rider can finish off the race.

Individual Sprint (Match Sprint)

A sprint race between two cyclists head-to-head over three laps of the track. The first part of the race can be very slow as both riders try to stay behind their opponent. In the last lap one rider suddenly makes a break, hoping to catch out his or her opponent. There is then a dramatic, high-speed sprint finish.

Keirin Another highly tactical race, this time for six to eight riders. This race starts with a series of laps in which the riders must stay behind a motorbike pacer called a **derny**. The derny gradually builds up speed. The riders try to get into the best position to take advantage of the moment when the derny pulls off the track. The last two-and-a-half laps are an all-out sprint to the finish line.

Time Trial, (1,000m men; 500m women) also called the Kilo. Riders begin from a standing start and ride against the clock. This is a high-pressure, one-off event timed to a 1,000th of a second. Riders need an explosive start and finish, but also require great endurance to keep up a high speed throughout all the laps.

Endurance events

Individual Pursuit (4,000m men; 3,000m women)

Two riders begin from a standing start on opposite sides of the track and 'pursue' each other. The winner is the person who either catches his or her opponent, or who covers the distance in the fastest time.

Team Pursuit (men only)

Two teams of four riders work tactically as a team. Each lead rider stays at the front for only a lap or so before leaving the main body, then re-joining at the back. The four team-mates ride close together and shield each other from wind resistance to save energy. The race time is taken as the third rider of each four-man team crosses the line, so the slowest rider in each team often drops out of the race altogether.

Points Race (40km men; 25km women)

The most tactical of all the races – a combination of speed and endurance. Points are awarded every ten laps to the first four riders to cross the line. If a rider manages to break away and **lap** the rest of the riders, he or she gains an extra ten points. At the end, the rider with the highest score wins.

Coach's notes: training

Strength, speed and power are essential to win races. But mental agility is just as important. Good riders win races in their heads as well as on the track.

Lines on the track

There are coloured lines on a velodrome track that section off various race areas. The black line is the most important as it marks the shortest distance around the track.

A four-man team take part in a Team Pursuit race.

Hannah concentrates hard as she takes part in an Individual Pursuit race.

Madison (50km – men only) Similar to the Points Race, but for two-man teams. Only one rider per team races at any time. The other rider circles the track high up on the banking, recovering his energy until he swoops down and is pulled back into the race by the racing rider. This handover is called a 'hand sling'. Points are scored for the first team past the line every 20 laps. This technical and tactical race can be very slow for large portions of the race, then accelerate to a highly charged sprint. Lapping the other teams can mean an outright win.

Scratch Race (usually 20km or 25km – men and women) The first over the line is the winner. There can be 30 or 40 riders on the track, all sprinting for the line.

Omnium (men and women) A track event with five different disciplines: a 200m flying-start Time Trial; a 5km Scratch Race; a 2km or 3km Individual Pursuit; a 15km Points Race; and a 1km Time Trial.

I compete in most of the track races. I am current title holder of the National U16 Scratch Race, Points Race, 500m Time Trial and the Sprint. I am more of an endurance rider, but have got a good sprint in me which comes in handy at the end of a race.

11

Road racing

Road racing is done on public roads or tarmac circuits. The lengths of the races vary enormously, from 20km for younger club riders to 200km races for elite riders.

What is a road race?

In a road race there can be more than 50 competitors all lining up to start at the same time. The first person over the finish line is the winner. The bit between is a mixture of endurance, sprinting and tactics. Riders have steep hills to climb up and speed down, an uneven tarmac surface and occasional bad weather to contend with. As well as cycling at speed throughout the race, they also need to save energy for a fast **sprint finish**.

Stage races

Some road races are done in stages over several days. Each stage has a winner. The **Tour de France** is the best known of the **stage races**. It lasts for three weeks.

Time trials

Time trials are races against the clock that take place on public roads. The riders start a minute apart. A time trial is known as the 'race of truth' because there's nowhere to hide – it's just you, the bike and the clock.

I prefer road racing to track racing because of the great variety in the courses. There is always something different to make the race interesting.

Lance Armstrong (left) of the USA, Bradley Wiggins (middle) and David Millar (right) of Great Britain climb a steep hill in the 2009 Tour de France.

Road bikes

Racing bikes built for the road have a lot of gears so that riders can choose the correct gear for the conditions. Riders hunch over the dropped handlebars to create as little wind resistance as possible. The tyres are thin and are kept at a high pressure.

Mountain bike racing

Mountain bike races are off-road races. They require exceptional bike-handling skills, as competitors negotiate jumps, bumps, banked corners (berms) and drop-offs (ledges with a drop on one side).

Cross-country

In a cross-country race all the riders start together. The route they follow is marked out. Each lap is typically between 3km and 6km. The length of the races vary. A top-level race will take two hours or longer.

Cross-country skills

To compete in cross-country mountain bike events, riders need a combination of endurance, fitness and bike-handling skills. If riders have bike problems they must do the repairs themselves, so they need some mechanical skills. On the track they have to negotiate tight turns, narrow, winding paths, rocks, tree roots and a range of other obstacles. The route will have hills and descents – and usually lots of mud!

Mountain bike cross-country is now an Olympic event for both men and women. In the Olympic Games the race distance is not fixed. It is decided the night before the race and depends on the weather. The officials set a course distance that they hope will give a race of about two hours and fifteen minutes for men, and two hours for women.

I like the fun of the rides and courses that we do in mountain biking. The social side of the events is good, too. When we go on camp we do workshops about bike mechanics and how to look after our bikes, including washing them after a race.

Alice takes to the air to avoid a hidden obstacle on this woodland track.

A downhill mountain bike race in action.

I compete in cross-country mountain bike races. I enjoy a cross session in the rain because you are always trying just to stay on the bike!

Coach's notes: mountain bike skills

Cross-country mountain bike races are not just about cycling well. Getting on and off and carrying the bike, all without losing time, are often important factors too.

Four cross (4X)

In 4X, four riders compete against each other at a time. The start is from behind a mechanical gate that drops down. The courses are quite short and mainly downhill. On the course there is a mixture of obstacles, some natural and some artificial. The winner is the first to cross the finish line.

Downhill

Riders race downhill individually against the clock. Races last between two and five minutes. On the course they face jumps, bumps, berms and drop-offs. The course can be very steep. Downhill racing is a test of the riders' nerves as well as their bike-handling.

Mountain bikes
Mountain bikes have strong, light frames, good brakes and lots of gears. Tyres are very broad and heavily knobbled. The riding position is quite upright so that riders can spot hazards coming up in front of them.

Cyclo-cross

Cyclo-cross began as a way of training to keep fit in the autumn and winter. It soon became popular as a sport in its own right, and races are held most weekends from November through to January.

In cyclo-cross racing, competitors navigate a range of different surfaces including woods, hills, grass and often mud.

The cyclists have artificial obstacles placed in their way. They have to dismount and carry their bikes round them.

Because of the terrain these races are not as fast as road races, but a cyclist's bike-handling skills are very important. Cyclo-cross racers also need great endurance.

Cyclo-cross races are usually not more than an hour long and consist of lots of laps of a short course, such as a park or playing field.

Hannah takes part in a very muddy National Trophy Cyclo-cross round.

Cyclo-cross bikes

Cyclo-cross bikes are similar to road bikes but they have thicker, stronger frames to withstand the rough conditions. The tyres have a lot of grip but are quite narrow in order to cut through the mud. These bikes have a lot of gears to cope with the hilly courses.

BMX

*Tre (left) races against his dad (second from right) and others in a **moto** at his local club.*

BMX (bicycle motocross) racing is a thrilling sport both to take part in and to watch. The races take place on outdoor circuits around 300m to 400m long. The circuits include jumps and banked corners. Up to eight riders take part in each race. The first over the finish line wins.

BMX clubs and tracks all over the country run training and racing for both kids and adults. At the elite level, BMX has been an Olympic event for both men and women since 2008.

A family sport

BMX riders start from as young as four years of age and continue into adulthood. Club races are grouped in ability and boys and girls race together. It is common for whole families to get involved in BMX. Parents who do not take part can help to score the races, act as mechanics, supply food and cheer on the competitors.

Flying through the air is quicker than pedalling around the track!

Tre rides around a berm at his local BMX track.

BMX bikes

BMX race bikes are very light. There is no front brake – only a back brake. There are no gears, so the rider has to pedal hard. The tyres are knobbly. There are two wheel sizes, the 24-inch cruiser and 20-inch racer.

BMX races

The start of a race is at the top of a steep slope. In top-level races there is an electronic gate that drops down in front of the riders. Getting a good start is essential to getting the best position on the track.

Races are run as a series of qualifying rounds called motos. The winners of the motos ride against each other to decide the finalists and an overall winner.

The races are very short – around 30 seconds long – and very fast. The riders take off over the bumps and aim for the best position on the berms. The riders are often close together in a pack, and accidents are common. If one rider falls, he or she often causes many others to go down too.

The best riders have the ability to pedal short distances with enormous power. They also need balance and stability to stay on the bike.

Coach's notes: attitude

After all the training the riders have put in, getting a gold medal in BMX racing at the Olympics will be down to a 30-second final. A rider has got to have the right attitude – keep cool and stay completely focused on the job.

The track at Peckham is much smaller than an international course. It is a very technical track to ride and everything is close together so you have to think really quickly. Riding a bigger course is easier once you get used to it.

In training

The type of training in a cyclist's programme varies according to the event for which he or she is preparing. Short, flat-out sprints require very different training from endurance events. Training programmes are designed to allow cyclists to peak at the right time for competitions.

The role of the coach

When a cyclist joins a club, his or her training will be organised by a coach. At the start, coaches train the cyclists in different types of cycling to find the one that suits them best. If they spot a talented rider who really wants to succeed they will help them to develop their potential on one of the programmes available (see page 7).

My dad takes me everywhere. Unfortunately there are only two indoor velodromes in the country (Newport in south Wales, and Manchester in northwest England), which means about one-and-a-half hours to Newport each way, and three hours to Manchester each way. I train six, sometimes seven, days a week. On average, my dad covers 30,000 miles (48,000km) a year taking me to and from training and racing.

John and his dad unpack the bikes to get ready for another training session.

Coach's notes: training

At the beginning of the year we decide which races to aim for. The training programme is then built around those races. There are smaller races as well to keep the cyclists competitive for the main races.

Training programme

A training programme is designed by a coach to achieve short-, medium- and long-term goals. It is different each day depending on the time of year and on the races a particular cyclist is training for. In the run-up to a big race, the coach gradually reduces the training to allow the cyclist's body to be able to perform at its best on the day. This is called **tapering**.

Mind training

Even the fittest cyclist can be beaten in a race by a lack of self-belief. The coach is responsible for **motivating** the cyclist and creating a strong belief that he or she can win. Specialist motivational coaches have had great success in training elite athletes in the art of winning.

The warm up

Cycling is very good all-round exercise, even for people not training at a high level. Cyclists do most of their training on the bike. Before they begin each training session, they must warm up their muscles and increase their heart rate. This is called a **cardiovascular warm up**. These exercises strengthen the heart and lungs and prepare the cyclist to work at maximum capacity during training. Having a strong heart and lungs enables a cyclist to use more oxygen and exercise more intensively without getting out of breath. It also increases the body's tolerance to **lactic acid** and adrenalin. These chemicals build up in the bloodstream and cause pain in the muscles when someone exercises very hard.

Tre warms up with a jog before training

*I always start with a 20-minute warm up and finish with a 10-minute **cool down**. Luckily I enjoy every aspect of my training, whether it be in the gym or on the track. I always give 110 per cent and sometimes I've put so much effort into the training session that I've been sick. (I don't like that too much.)*

Endurance training

Riders need lots of stamina to compete in endurance events. They also need to be able to conserve enough energy for a tactical sprint within the race and a sprint finish. The outcome of a long race may be decided in the last few metres and won by the competitor who is capable of an explosive burst of speed. Cyclists need to be super-fit but not heavy – there must be a balance between building muscle and staying lean. Endurance training is done on the bike by cycling for periods of time, gradually building up to the distance of the race, and also doing high-intensity sprints.

Portable rollers allow cyclists to train on the track, the road or even in the living room!

Sprint training

Sprint races need explosive power and then... even more explosive power! Powerful legs are essential for working at a very high speed for a short time. A sprint cyclist's upper body strength must also be good for balance.

I try to get to the gym twice a week. I do exercises for both my upper and lower body. I also stretch a lot after gym and track training to try to keep supple and help prevent injury.

These exercises for leg strength (left) and upper body/back strength (right) are suitable for both sprint and BMX training.

Tre finds a quiet stretch of road near his home to do a training session.

My main training session of the week is on Saturday at the BMX track. My coach, CK Flash, runs the session. Other than that I do most of my training on the roads near where I live. I try to get to the gym as often as I can, too.

I train six or seven days a week. All my training is on the bike, I don't train in the gym. Most of the training is done on the roads around where I live.

BMX training

BMX races are short, but very fast. Riders' training concentrates on being able to pump the legs very fast and keep perfect balance while negotiating the banks and bumps on the course. As well as road and race training, BMX riders work with weights in the gym to improve their leg and upper body strength.

Cool down

At the end of a session, riders do a series of stretches to cool down. These stretches are done while the rider is still (**static stretches**). Static stretches allow the muscles to relax and prevent them from stiffening up and causing **cramp**. They also help the riders to keep supple and avoid getting injured.

*Alice and Hannah have **satellite navigation** systems attached to their bikes so they don't get lost on long training rides.*

Lifestyle

It takes talent to become a professional sports person – and it also takes great dedication. Reaching the top of any sport involves years of training, travelling, watching your diet and leading a healthy lifestyle.

My headteacher lets me go out training when it can be fitted into my timetable.

Academic work

Cycling coaches understand how important academic studies are for their riders and build time into their training plans for homework. Schools are usually proud of their pupils' sporting achievements, and help them to fit their training into their timetables.

Diet

Cyclists need to be light, but very strong. The amount of training they do means that they do not usually need to restrict the amount of food they eat, but they must eat the right sort of food. Five portions of fruit and vegetables a day help to provide the required **nutrients** and **minerals**. A high-**carbohydrate** and low-fat intake is also necessary to give the body the energy to train well each day.

I avoid fizzy drinks as they can make lactic acid build up in your muscles. I don't eat chips or fatty food.

Injuries

All sports have some degree of risk, and cycling is no exception. When you are racing at speed only a few centimetres away from your team-mates in a Team Pursuit, it takes only

I had a fall and broke my wrist in three places when I was racing in Manchester. It took me six weeks to get fit enough to start racing again.

Tre's mum packs him a lunch to make sure he is not tempted by unhealthy foods.

a slight loss of concentration to cause a pile-up. Mountain biking and road racing can also have particularly dramatic spills. Good safety equipment makes the sport as safe as possible. Warming up and cooling down helps cyclists to avoid muscle strains and pulls.

Social life

Dedicating yourself to a sport at a young age can mean missing out on leisure time and seeing friends. The riders in this book feel that achieving their goals will make up for any sacrifices they have to make.

Cyclists on one of the development programmes attend regular training camps. These camps are great places to make friends with others who share a love of cycling.

Travel

Attending training camps and taking part in international competitions can give young riders opportunities to travel all over the world. All the riders featured in the book have had experiences of racing or training abroad.

Sometimes it would be nice to go out with friends at a weekend, but I know I have to stay focused and remain on track to fulfil my dream of being an Olympic champion.

I have trained in Majorca and the Netherlands. I've also raced in Holland and Belgium.

I don't miss out on too much – maybe the odd party. I enjoy cycling so much that my leisure time is my cycling competitions. We spent a week at camp in Assen, in the Netherlands, and I took part in a youth stage race. Things like that make up for a lot.

I have raced in Denmark and Belgium. In November 2009 I went to Tulsa, USA, to race at the American Bicycle Association (ABA) finals. I made it to the final in my age group, and came fifth.

Races

The preparation for a competition is both physical and mental. The training for a big race is designed so that riders are at the peak of their physical and mental fitness at just the right moment.

Saving energy

Winning a race is not just about cycling as fast as possible for the whole race. Long races are won or lost by how well a rider paces him or herself. Burning up all your energy by going too fast at the start of a race may mean being overtaken on the finish line. On the other hand, if you still have energy left after the end of a race, you probably could have gone faster.

Tactics

Track races are very tactical. A rider will have worked out his or her own race plan, but riders need to be able to rethink these plans quickly as things change around them. They also need fast reactions to keep up with riders who break away from the pack.

For track events, particularly the sprint events, I watch a lot of DVDs, which I get from my coach. I've also learned a lot from watching the seniors racing. You learn from experience too. You try some different tactics – some work and some don't.

The rainbow jersey
The reigning world champion in any type of cycling wears a white jersey with five coloured stripes (green, yellow, black, red and blue). It is known as the 'rainbow jersey'. In stage races, the leader wears a coloured jersey so that he or she can be easily seen. In the Tour de France it is the famous yellow jersey.

Hannah wears a yellow jersey as she wins Round 4 of the Cyclo-cross National Trophy in 2009.

Alice enjoys her victory in a round of the National Points mountain bike series in Dalby Forest, Yorkshire.

I've done so many races now I can't really remember what it felt like to compete for the first time – but I was probably in the wrong gear!

Race day

All the weeks and months of training are put to the test on the day of a big race. The cyclists taper their training before the race (see page 19) so that they are rested and ready to perform. Some athletes have a particular routine before a race to bring them luck. They eat the same things, or listen to certain pieces of music.

The cyclists gradually warm up their muscles, just as they do before training. They might run through their race plan and tactics with their coach. Those that suffer from nerves may work on keeping a positive and focused approach to the race. After all – the race is up to them to win or lose.

John enjoys the applause from the crowd after winning a race.

The adrenalin-rush when you know you have set a fast time, and the applause from the spectators when you win a race are what make all the training worth it.

Sporting heroes

Top-level cyclists are heroes for the many fans of the sport. They are an inspiration to young people starting out in the sport, and their conduct sets an example for others to follow.

Young British cyclists do not have to look far for inspiration. British cyclists won 14 medals at the Beijing Olympics in 2008, eight of them gold.

Olympic gold medallists Chris Hoy and Victoria Pendleton celebrate their wins during Britain's Olympic medal winners' parade in London, 2008.

Team GB cycling medals Olympic Games 2008

Gold
*Nicole Cooke (Road race)
Chris Hoy, Jamie Staff and Jason Kenny (Team Sprint)
Bradley Wiggins (Individual Pursuit)
Chris Hoy (Keirin)
Rebecca Romero (Individual Pursuit)
Ed Clancy, Paul Manning, Geraint Thomas and Bradley Wiggins (Team Pursuit)
Victoria Pendleton (Sprint)
Chris Hoy (Sprint)*

Silver
*Emma Pooley (Time Trial)
Ross Edgar (Keirin)
Wendy Houvenaghel (Individual Pursuit)
Jason Kenny (Sprint)*

Bronze
*Chris Newton (Points Race)
Steven Burke (Individual Pursuit)*

Sir Chris Hoy
*Great Britain
Date of birth: 23 March 1976
2008 Olympic Games: Gold – Keirin, Gold – Men's Sprint, Gold – Team Sprint*

2008 World Track Championships: Gold – Keirin, Gold – Men's Sprint, Silver – Team Sprint

2007 World Track Championships: Gold – Keirin, Gold – Men's Kilo Time Trial, Silver – Team Sprint

Victoria Pendleton
*Great Britain
Date of birth: 24 Sept 1980
2008 Olympic Games: Gold – Women's Sprint*

2008 World Track Championships: Gold – Women's Team Sprint (with Shanaze Reade), Gold – Women's Sprint, Silver – Keirin

2007 World Track Championships: Gold – Women's Team Sprint (with Shanaze Reade), Gold – Women's Sprint, Gold – Women's Keirin

I admire Craig MacLean and Chris Hoy. They are friendly and humble. They train hard to win and have determination.

I first met them at a sprint school at Newport in Wales and we hit it off from the start – they are both Scottish, and so am I, so there was a connection! They were great in encouraging me on the track and I remember learning loads from them on the day.

Since then Craig has given me one-to-one coaching in the gym, as well as advice for the explosive starts needed for being rider 1 on the Team Sprint.

I admire Lance Armstrong because he had cancer and has fought it to come back into the sport.

I have been to Majorca training with Malcolm Elliott. Everything he did was very precise and he took the training seriously. I admire him because he has been competitive in the cycling world for a long time.

Mike Day (left) and Donny Robinson (right) from the United States compete in the quarterfinals of the UCI BMX Supercross World Cup.

Mike Day
USA
Date of birth: 9 Oct 1984

2008 Olympic Games: Silver
UCI BMX Supercross World Cup:
2007 Gold, 2004 Silver
UCI BMX World Championships:
2006 Bronze, 2005 Silver

The American BMX rider Mike Day is ranked number one in the world. He's the rider I most want to be like.

Plans and ambitions

Making a career as an elite cyclist requires dedication, skill and talent. Some cyclists continue to compete at a high level well into their thirties. When they do retire, many continue with a career in coaching, passing their skills on to another generation of cyclists.

Olympic gold

For all sportsmen and women there is something very special about representing your country in international competitions. Winning a gold medal at the Olympic Games, held every four

My ambition in cycling is to become a professional cyclist and become Olympic, World and Commonwealth champion for the Sprint.

Over the next two years I will work hard on the Olympic Development Programme. I aim to win the junior National Sprint Championship and also be junior European and World Sprint and Keirin champion.

I will also need a bit of luck to stay healthy and injury-free.

When I give up competing, I'd love to continue in the sport and coach. I'd like to give something back to the sport and hopefully find a talented young person who would then go on to be a World or Olympic champion. That would be awesome!

John already has an impressive array of gold medals. He is training hard in the hope that he can add an Olympic gold to his collection.

My aim is to win an Olympic BMX gold medal for Great Britain. If I had to give up because I got injured, I would stay in BMX and become a coach.

In five year's time I would like to train at the U23 Academy. To do that I need to keep working hard and get some experience of racing abroad.

If I had to give up cycling for some reason, I would like to be a sports teacher in a secondary school.

My ultimate ambition has to be to represent my country at the Olympics and win Olympic gold!

years, is the dream for all competitive cyclists. Mountain biking, road racing, track and BMX are all Olympic sports for both men and women.

Other competitions

As well as the Olympic Games, different types of cycling have their own top international competitions. There are competitions to aim for in track, cyclo-cross, road, BMX and mountain biking, as well as many other national and international events.

In road racing, the three **grand tours** (Tour de France, **Giro d'Italia** and **Vuelta a España**), held in France, Italy and Spain respectively, are high on the list for riders.

John, Hannah, Tre and Alice have already shown that they have talent and dedication. If they have the perseverence to continue, we wish them luck in achieving their ambitions.

Hannah already knows what it feels like to cross the finish line ahead of the rest of the pack. Maybe one day she will do it at a World Championship or at the Olympic Games.

Glossary

adrenalin A hormone that is released into the bloodstream in response to physical or mental stress. It stimulates the body to perform at its maximum level.

aerodynamic Something designed to have the least wind resistance possible.

aerodynamic drag The difference in air pressure in front of and behind a cyclist that pulls him or her back.

air pressure The weight of the air pushing on a surface.

bicycle motocross (BMX) A style of off-road racing on tracks that contain jumps and other hazards.

carbohydrates A group of foods that includes sugars and starches.

cardiovascular The system that carries blood to and from all parts of the body.

cool down Exercises done after training to relax the muscles and prevent cramp.

cramp A sudden, sometimes painful, contraction of a muscle.

cyclo-cross A type of cycle race in which competitors navigate different surfaces and artificial obstacles placed in their way.

derny A motorbike pacer that riders must stay behind in the first part of a Keirin race.

elite A group of people who are at the top level in their sport.

endurance The ability to exercise for a long time without getting tired.

fixed wheel A type of bicycle used for track cycling. Whenever the bicycle is moving the pedals are also going round.

four-cross (4X) A type of short, downhill, cross-country mountain bike race where four riders compete against each other at one time.

gear A device that controls how much power goes from the pedals to the wheels of a bicycle.

Giro d'Italia A long-distance road stage race held in Italy. It is one of three races that together are called the 'grand tours'.

grand tours The three long-distance road cycle races in France (Tour de France), Italy (Giro d'Italia), and Spain (Vuelta a España).

Individual Sprint (Match Sprint) A sprint race between two cyclists head-to-head over three laps of the track.

Keirin An individual track cycling race. The race starts with a series of laps in which the riders must stay behind a motorbike pacer called a derny.

Kilo (Time Trial) An individual track cycle race. The fastest rider wins.

lactic acid A substance produced in the muscles during exercise. Too much lactic acid can cause cramping pains.

lap When a rider laps another rider in a race, it means that he or she is ahead by one whole lap of the track.

Madison A track cycling event for two-man teams. Riders are awarded points as they race. The team with the highest score wins.

minerals Elements in food such as calcium, iron, magnesium, potassium and sodium. They are essential for our bodies to function correctly.

moto The qualifying races in a BMX competition.

motivating Helping and encouraging.

nutrients The substances in food that are used by the body to grow and stay healthy.

Points Race An individual track cycling event. Riders are awarded points as they race. At the end the rider with the highest score wins.

satellite navigation A system for finding directions using orbiting satellites.

sprint To move very fast for a short distance.

sprint finish A burst of speed at the end of a race towards the finishing line.

stage race A long cycle race that is split into a series of smaller races called 'stages'.

stamina The ability to exercise intensely for a long period of time.

static stretch A stretching exercise done whilst remaining in one place.

taper The gradual reduction of the level of training before a competition.

Team Sprint A race where teams of three enter, but only one rider finishes.

Tour de France A long-distance road stage race held in France. It is one of three races that together are called the 'grand tours'.

velodrome An indoor wooden cycle racing arena with sloping sides, used for track cycle races.

Vuelta a España A long-distance road stage race held in Spain. It is one of three races that together are called the 'grand tours'.

warm up To do gentle exercises to warm the muscles before training.

wind resistance The force of the air pushing against something while it is travelling.

Find out more

Websites

http://new.britishcycling.org.uk/
The official site for cycling in Great Britain. This site is packed with interesting information for any cycling enthusiast whatever type of cycling it is that you are interested in. Read about the 'rising stars' in cycling, get up to date with Team GB and the Olympic news and catch up with all the latest results in your favourite cycling events.

http://www.welshcycling.co.uk/
The official site for cycling in Wales.

http://www.britishcycling.org.uk/web/site/SCU/scuhome/sc_home.asp
Scottish Cycling official site.

Books

Know Your Sport: Cycling (Franklin Watts, 2008)
This book contains a lot of general information as well as step-by-step photographs. Profiles and statistics give information about some of the world's greatest cyclists.

Index

4X (four cross) 14

aerodynamics 8
ambitions 28–9
Armstrong, Lance 12, 27

bike mechanics 13
Bikeability 6
bikes 8, 12, 14, 15, 17
BMX (bicycle motocross) 6,
    16–17, 27
BMX training 20, 21

cardiovascular warm up 19
clubs 6–7, 16
coaches 18, 19
competitions 7, 28
cooling down 21, 23
cross-country 13
cyclo-cross 15

Day, Mike 27
derny 9
diet 22
downhill racing 14

Elliott, Malcolm 27
endurance events 8, 10–11
endurance training 20
exercises 19, 20, 21

Giro d'Italia 29
Go-Ride 7
grand tours 29

hand sling 11
helmets 8

heroes 26–7
Hoy, Sir Chris 26, 27

Individual Pursuit 10, 11
Individual Sprint 8, 9
injuries 22–3

Keirin 9
Kilo 4, 9

lifestyle 22–3

MacLean, Craig 27
Madison 11
Match Sprint 9
Millar, David 12
mind training 10, 19
mountain bike racing
    13–14, 23, 25

Olympic Development
    Programme 7
Olympic Games 4, 13, 16,
    17, 26, 27, 28, 29
Olympic Podium Programme
    7
Omnium 11

Pendleton, Victoria 26
Points Race 10

races 24–5
rainbow jersey 24
road racing 12, 23
Robinson, Donny 27
rollers 20

school 6, 22
Scratch Race 11
social life 23
sprint events 8–9, 25
sprint finish 12, 20
sprint training 20
stage races 12
static stretches 21

tactics 24
Talent Team Programme 7
tapering 19, 25
Team Pursuit 10, 22–3
Team Sprint 8–9
Time Trial (Kilo) 4, 9
time trials (road) 12
Tour de France 12, 24, 29
track cycling 8–9, 10–11,
    24
tracks 8, 10
training 10, 18–19, 20–1
training camps 7, 23
travel 23

U23 Academy Programme
    7

velodromes 8, 10, 18
Vuelta a España 29

warming up 19, 23, 25
Wiggins, Bradley 12, 26